DUCKS FOR STARTERS

A PRACTICAL GUIDE TO BACKYARD DUCK KEEPING

BRUCE WICKING

First published 1990. Reprinted 2021

Copyright © 2021 Richard Lee Publishing

Back over duck photograph courtesy of Amanda Palmer.

Excerpts from the poem *Ducks* by F. W. Harvey taken from *Feet on the Ground* Blackie and Son 1950

ISBN: 978-0-909431-18-1

❀ Created with Vellum

FEET ON THE GROUND

BY F. W. HARVEY

From the troubles of the world
I turn to ducks,
Beautiful comical things
Sleeping or curled
Their heads beneath white wings
By water cool
Or finding curious things
To eat in various mucks
Beneath the pool.

All God's jokes are good – even the practical ones! And as for the duck, I think God must have smiled a bit, seeing those bright eyes blink on the day He fashioned it. And He's probably laughing still at the sound that came out of its bill!

FOREWORD

When my sister-in-law presented me with a Muscovy drake and four ducks of various ages, I shut them in the only available enclosure, the chicken pen. By next morning they had emptied the hens water bucket, trampled on two eggs and the drake was eyeing off several young pullets. It was time to seek enlightenment.

WHAT SORT OF DUCKS

THE MUSCOVY / THE KHAKI CAMPBELL / DUAL-PURPOSE DUCKS / KEEPING A MIXED FLOCK

If you are starting from scratch, you will probably have mulled over the arguments for keeping ducks. Space maybe you are looking for meat birds, maybe you want eggs, or the snails massacred. Maybe would like ducks around as an interest for the kids or just because ducks appeal to you.

For all practical purposes there are two types of duck, the White Muscovy and the rest. Of the rest, Khaki Campbells are probably the most common. There is no reason why you should not keep more than one variety at the same time, but it is worth being aware of some of the complexities that can crop up, particularly if space is limited.

When people come to use us to buy ducks, I ask them "what kind of dark did you have in mind?" Sometimes the answer is quite decided. "Give me Muscovies. I can't stand those mad Campbells." or, "Kaki Campbells please; Muscovies are so dull and uninteresting."

Once people have kept their first lot of ducks, they expect them all to be similar and it comes as a shock when they switch from the placid Muscovy to the volatile Khaki Campbell, or vice versa. If they had purchased geese, they would have expected differences. We recently took delivery of a new puppy after our old faithful had come off second best in an encounter with a truck. This pup is different; it has different eating and sleeping habits; it has different resting sites, different play behaviour and greets visitors more exuberantly. It is also more active than its aged predecessor.

Now we expected it to be different; we approached it tentatively and the pup learnt 'do's' and 'dont's'.

Although some of the rules have not changed, a new pup is a new ball game and I don't leave my shoes on the veranda floor any more.

If you acquire ducks, observe them, and give them time to become accustomed to you and to their new environment. They will produce more eggs, they will be contented and grow faster, their young will be more manageable and you will enjoy keeping them.

So, what are ducks like? How should we expect them to behave? Most notably in our community birds, not only as youngsters, but in maturity. Fights and even scraps among ducks of the one species are rare, and there is not the same aggressive pecking order that is evident with chickens. New ducks (of a similar age) are easily excepted and integrate with the rest of the flock quickly.

Which Duck should I buy?

THE MUSCOVY

That Muscovy is named after the Musk duck from Brazil and is often regarded as a goose rather than a duck. It differs from other ducks in a number of aspects and its origins suggest explanations for temperament and behavioural differences.

- The Muscovy is a meat bird and it lays only to hatch young.
- It is not suited to confined areas as it makes a mess

around the back door and often flies during the adolescent phase.
- It is tractable, placid and does not wander far.
- Two females would make satisfactory pets, though not in a cuddly way.

The placid Muscovy.

- Eggs hatch in 35 days. You can expect two hatchings a year, maybe three from younger ducks and one from the older ladies, though when they do make the effort, they sally forth with rejuvenated spirit. The best ducks will produce an early clutch, maturing for Christmas eating, the second will be ready for Easter and a third for winter.
- In Australia, laying commences about July, and goes through to about March, and from the age of about 8 to 12 months.

———

THE KHAKI CAMPBELL

The Khaki Campbell and the Muscovy are the most commonly kept breeds; Muscovy for the table and the Khaki Campbell for eggs.

- The Khaki Campbell is an excellent layer, producing some 200 to 300 eggs per year. (The Indian Runner would be runner-up in egg production with only a slightly lower number of eggs per year. The other less popular breeds would produce about half that number.)
- They quack, at least the females do, whereas the Muscovy confines its communications to sibilant hisses.
- They make good eating, though they are much smaller than the Muscovy and their flesh is darker.
- They lay most of the year round.
- They can go clucky towards the end of their laying season; some feel maternal much earlier but can be discouraged if eggs are removed each day.
- They are sociable, gregarious and 'hyperactive', great roamers and death to snails.
- Though not as tame as the Muscovy, the Khaki Campbell settle quickly if kept in small numbers and they are happy in a good sized back yard providing there are snails to hunt and vegetation to explore. I have heard of some pairs which have stayed very close to the home shed for up to 3–4 weeks before plucking up courage to venture fourth.
- Laying commences around May in Australia, though you would not expect much from them before 8 months of age.
- Eggs hatch in 28 days.

––––––––

DUAL-PURPOSE DUCKS

Their are other varieties of ducks which can just as easily grace the home poultry flock. Among these are the *Pekin* (a white duck), the *Rouen* and the *Indian Runner* to mention the best known, along with the *Cayuga* and the *Aylesbury* (another white bird). All varieties are fed and managed in a similar manner.

If you are looking for a dual-purpose duck, one that lays a modest 150 to 200 eggs a year and throws a heavy quick maturing youngster, then so are we all. The current commercial wisdom is that the *Pekin* is the closest to the ideal. If you possess the right strain of meat bird, maturity can be achieved in nine weeks. However, ducks bought at the supermarket are usually size 13, or 1.3kg., a size suited to the restaurant market rather than the home table and less than half the weight of a Muscovy drake at 16 weeks.

KEEPING A MIXED FLOCK

Ducks of different breeds can quite happily share an area. Whether you stick to the one breed or find yourself with a few of this and a few of that, the following hints should prove useful.

A mixed flock home for dinner

- Females of all varieties live together peaceably, though they do not mix socially.
- Drakes are in no way necessary nor helpful to induce laying. They simply fertilise eggs!
- Drake to duck ratio should be from 1 to 4 and up to 1 to 8. Ducks can suffer considerable harassment if the ratio is too low and Muscovy ducks will

sometimes fly off to escape. There is absolutely no virtue in keeping a drake unless you wish to set eggs. The drake eats pellets for no reason and, if you live in a town, the chased ducks can keep the neighbours awake.

- One alternative to the drake-duck problem is to either borrow a drake when you want some fertility or buy one and eat it when its mission is completed. You could of course purchase fertile eggs and slip them under the duck when she commences sitting. Her own eggs can be removed and should be quite edible if you make the switch in the first 24 hours.

- If you bring in a drake, you should expect to wait one week before being reasonably certain that the ducks are laying fertile eggs.

- In the rare case of a mishap and you are left with only one duck, it should be eaten or taken to another flock.

- In particular, a drake will exhibit bizarre behaviour if deprived of company. A neighbours drake, a solitary bird following the despatch of his harem, pulled out feathers and dashed itself against its reflection in the glass door of the house. When it was eventually placed with our ducks, it returned to normal immediately.

- Ponds are not necessary, but water deep enough to immerse their heads in should be available to your ducks at all times. Experience will tell you how much water can be used in one day. Ducks use the water, not only for drinking, but to clear their nasal passages and to maintain eye hygiene. An infection known as White Eye is spread very quickly through dirty watering sites.

- Ducks can be a threat to a garden, no matter how large. Some vegetables are irresistible and damp spots invite deep beak exploration. It is well worth having a few metres of wire netting and some posts or stands so that you can quickly set up a 'no-go' area as circumstance require.

- Muscovies and others will co-exist, although I always separate them at night. A Khaki Campbell drake should always be with his own ducks or he will breed with the Muscovies, edging out the Muscovy drake and siring only 'mules' to show for it. (Mules are the non-fertile progeny of animals or birds of the same family but of separate breeds, e.g. the offspring of a donkey crossed with a horse or that of a canary crossed with a goldfinch. This is most rare among wild animals but less so with domestic stock. You can't breed from mules.)

- By separating Muscovies from Khaki Campbells (and I usually apply this to other varieties also), it is more peaceful and it prevents the chaos that can arise when cluckies lay in each other's nests and sit on the wrong eggs, or worse still, sit on a mixture of eggs which hatch a week apart.

- Laying and breeding performances decline after the second year.

———

2

HOUSING

NATURAL SHELTER / FENCES / LAYING SITES / FLOORS, SMELLS AND OTHER THINGS

So you have decided on the type of duck you prefer. Next question, "Where shall I put them?"

There is no question that ducks should be allowed to roam during the day. They are natural grazers, they enjoy fossicking, and why pay for feed when they enjoy find their own feed for free? If you cannot let them roam, then you should keep chickens instead.

Unfortunately, yarding them with fowls is not satisfactory, though if you only have a pair and you let them out every morning, the problems are minor unless fighting breaks out. What happens is that the ducks dirty the water and saturate the surrounds; they matt the surface litter, creating soggy areas which harbour intestinal worms, serious in fowls, though the ducks seem to be very resistant. Ducks can also be intimidated by the more aggressive chickens and they have few answers to sharp beaks. A Khaki Campbell drake however, can shatter the tranquility in any chook yard. I have always provided separate overnight yarding and shelter. Undoubtedly, birds prefer to with others of their own breed and at best, tolerate the close proximity of different breeds and other fowl.

A 3 metre x 3 metre shed will provide overnight accomodation for up to six or eight ducks, assuming they are let out first thing in the morning and not locked up till dusk. If they are free range, they might not return home till sunset anyway. I let ours out each morning around 7.30 as egg laying is usually completed by then, though I occasionally find an egg in the grass in the late afternoon.

If you have between ten and twenty ducks and a 6 metre by 3 metre yard, it is worth constructing a decent shelter. Several galvanised water tanks cut in half can provide instant accomodation, but there are drawbacks. Tanks are quite adequate for most of the year, but problems commence when the winter rains set in. The run-off creates puddles and water often seeps into the nests. Also, half-tanks are low, and while it's OK retrieving eggs during the summer, come winter, you will soon become fed up with wet knees and mucky hands. Whatever type of shelter you build, make sure that you seal up holes. Ducks are hardy and can with stand the cold, but like all domestic livestock, drafts cause them much discomfort and eventually ill-health.

NATURAL SHELTER

Shrubbery in the yard is appreciated, though it needs to be non-edible. I have planted a few New Zealand flax plants, five in a clump with one metre spacing between clumps. They provide excellent shade, laying sites for the ducks and resting area and hideaways for chooks and hatchlings of all species, and even the lambs. All birds need ready access to hidey-holes so they can feel secure when resting and where they can escape the notice of older birds, aggressive siblings or the ubiquitous hawk.

We have also planted fruit trees in the yard. The fowls provide all the necessary fertiliser, though they also pull leaves off any branch within leaping distance. Wire netting guards during the green months are the only answer, at least until the trees have gained some height.

FENCES

A one metre high fence will restrain Khaki Campbells which do not fly, and usually Muscovies, though a two metre fence is required to exclude predators, particularly dogs and foxes. If the whim takes them, Muscovies will fly, certainly during adolescence. They will walk on roofs and perch on chimneys in the early morning and they take to the air to escape the attention of the drake who is permanently grounded.

———

LAYING SITES

Ducks will lay their eggs anywhere, unless broody. Provide some scrapes of hollows and lined with a little straw or dry grass and cap them with upturned wooden fruit boxes (if they are available) with one side removed. This usually persuades them to lay their eggs where they can be easily recovered and without too much mud adhering to them. They will also be better protected from crows and other egg eating birds. Muscovies also need boxes, upright partitions or lean-to's as cubbies for nests. A hay bale leaning against a wall is ideal.

———

FLOORS, SMELLS AND OTHER THINGS

Concrete or brick floors are considered too hard on a duck's feet unless a covering of shavings is applied. I have paved sections of the yard so that I can collect eggs in winter without slipping over or losing a rubber boot. I apply a 5 centimetres layer of sawdust-shavings under the covered areas. These days it is worth checking that the shavings do not include those from treated pine which contains traces of the heavy metal, cadmium; not recommended in a duck's diet!

If you use wire netting around the yard, you will need to take precautions to prevent hatchlings from squeezing through. A 150 mm strip of small gauge wire netting or some old boards will do the job.

Smells from the duck-yard are a sure sign that the area needs some attention. I suggest that you review the following:

- The number of ducks to the size of the yard or shedding.
- Whether there is an adequate supply of dry litter.
- The frequency of attention given to the litter, i.e. turning, adding to, or changing it.
- The design of drainage and run off areas and control of water spillage.

Just outside of the town where we live on Victoria's south-west coast, it is best if shelters face the north or north-east. This positioning fends of the prevailing south-westerlies and gives the sun a chance to dry off the floor each day.

Remember, it can become very hot on some summer days, particularly under a low tin roof, so provide protection for nesting birds, branches, wet bags or anything which can screen out some of the direct sunlight hitting the iron.

———

3

FEEDING

FEEDING DUCKLINGS / FEEDING ADULTS / FATTENING DUCKS / SHELLGRIT / FEEDING AFTERTHOUGHTS

Feeding is the least of your problems when you keep ducks. A few years ago a feeding mash had to be studied for balance and mixed daily. Nowadays, pellets do the job and you are ill advised if you scorn this product of modern technology. Ducks enjoy a little grain for variety and need daily access to pasture, greens and shellgrit.

FEEDING DUCKLINGS

Ducklings are unable to eat pellets or whole grain in the first few weeks, so stock feed manufacturers market proprietary brands of crumbles or chick-bits. These are ideal for hatchlings in their first 4 to 6 weeks. These may be replaced in part by other grains, preferably crushed wheat or barley, but only if extra protein can be provided in the form of meat meal, worms or meat scraps. Protein is essential for the growth of young birds, especially as their feathers are almost pure protein. The proprietary feeds also contain coccidiostat which controls bacterial scours or diarrhoea, a totally avoidable infection.

I supply only chick-bits for the first few days so that a taste is well acquired. Pellets and grain in a taller container are provided for and appreciated by mum. After 3 or 4 days, I introduce them to some bread in the water and they begin to enjoy greens such as lettuce and young silver beet. For up to a month, the overnight ration is chick-bits only or, chick-bits with a little cracked grain. This ensures that they gain nourishment, even if they fill up on scraps during the day or are edged out of delicacies such as worms and beetles, by older birds or stronger siblings.

Healthy ducklings busy feeding.

Starter pellets (high protein pellets) can then be used through till 4 or 5 months, though they are more expensive than layer pellets. Layer pellets are quite satisfactory providing you are able to supply the young ducklings with extra protein.

––––––

FEEDING THE ADULTS

Adult ducks forage for most of their food and they should obtain their basic diet from the area where they roam. Unless you have too many birds, sufficient green food is usually obtained in the garden, but if ducks are roaming a paddock, pasture needs to be watered regularly so that succulent young grass is constantly available. Rank grass, even though green, is of little nutritional value and in fact is usually ignored by the ducks.

I always supplement their foraging with overnight feed in the form of laying pellets, grain and scraps; this maintains egg production and increases the size of eggs. Our eggs usually weigh between 100 and 120 grams, though one tipped the scales at 200 grams. The mere sight of it brought water to my eyes.

Pellets must be kept dry. If by chance rain or other water gets to them, mix them with scraps in a mash immediately, otherwise they will go mouldy. Pellet powder from the bottom of the bag can also be mixed into the mash. Potatoes and hard vegetables should be boiled until soft. Mouldy scraps, especially bread, can kill ducks.

Ducks rejoice in wet weather when they find plenty of worms and insects, but com the dry, they are dependent on us for a greater percentage of their rations. Resign yourself to paying out more for feed as summer takes over. When scavenging is poor, our ducks soon let us know; they head for home much earlier, they yell at the back gate and follow at heel if I venture outside. Khaki Campbells roam further as they grow older, but Muscovies are more homebound.

———

FATTENING DUCKS

I take no special steps to fatten Khaki Campbells, but Muscovy drakelets consume prodigious quantities of food, and if they are to be fattened, you will need to supplement the pellets and grain with bread and scraps mixed with meatmeal. Add meatmeal at about 10% by weight. Because they are sedentary creatures there is little to be gained by confining them in the hope that they will maintain or gain weight.

———

SHELLGRIT

Sand and shellgrit help digestion and ensure strong egg shells. Egg shells are almost pure calcium and this comes from crushed mollusc shells we buy as shellgrit. With the high egg-producing Khaki Campbell, availability of this item is very important. Pellets contain some calcium but not enough for productive ducks. Occasionally I find an egg in the grass, usually late in the afternoon. Almost always the shell is missing. I never know whether a duck has laid a second egg or whether a lack of calcium in her system has delayed laying.

———

FEEDING AFTERTHOUGHTS

Chicken laying pellets are usually used for ducks, though duck pellets are obtainable from some grain stores. Pellets come in 40kg bags as do chick-bits or crumbles, but if you are running only a few ducks or have just one clutch of ducklings, then it would be better to buy in smaller lots as the pellets deteriorate after a month, vitamins in particular being affected.

Khaki Campbells are often kept to tackle snails, an excellent source of protein, but watch them; they are death to the garden pests but are also fatal to lettuce and silver beet and any other tiny plants and seedlings can suffer from nonchalant pecks in passing.

If your ducks are suspicious of new food, serve it in water. I often tip whole wheat grain into a rubbish bin lid or shallow tin of water. This entices the ducks and deters the other fowls and wild birds.

Feeding late in the day targets the feed accurately and deprives the sparrows and other robbers of an opportunity to escalate your food bill.

4

WATER

WATER - THE VITAL ELEMENT / RECEPTACLES / THE POND / HYPOTHERMIA IN DUCKLINGS

WATER - THE VITAL ELEMENT

You can provide inadequate housing; you can experiment with their feed; you can forget to let them out in the morning; you can make mistakes and get away with them, BUT, ducks will not forgive you if they are deprived of water. Forgetting the water is a cardinal sin of omission.

First and foremost, ducks are water birds and are only happy if they have access to water. They also need water to assist in digestion if it is not available, the food clogs in the oesophagus. Older ducks will be distressed but recover from discomfiture, but in ducklings, an extended oesophagus with attendant wind and indigestion, leads to deformed bodies, no growth and an early death. It is not commonly realised that unlike chickens, ducks do not have a 'crop' where food is ground and prepared for digestion. Instead, they rely on water to ease the food into their stomachs.

If by accident or error, the water cans are dry and the ducks or ducklings are hungry, do not feed them until you have given them a drink.

Make sure then, that your water receptacles are more than

ample in size, that water is replenished and replaced regularly and that, during summer at least, some water is located in the shade as warm water is not acceptable. It is a good idea to site food and water containers some distance apart so that crowding is reduced and feed can be kept dry.

RECEPTACLES

For water vessels for ducklings, I save or scrounge plastic ice cream containers, cut them down to about 5 centimetres in height and tack them to a wooden board to prevent them capsizing. These containers hold water well and, if they do eventually leak, they can be used for feed. The problem is that ducklings climb in, splash the water about and empty the container. To counter this and provide a cleaner water supply, invest in commercially available bottle and tray water containers, or make your own. I take a plastic soft-drink bottle and drill several 3 or 4 millimetre holes down close to the base, fill it with water, replace the cap and stand it in the ice cream container. (Make sure the top of the holes in the bottle are below the height of the walls of the container.) Until the ducklings are old enough to knock over the bottle, this reservoir provides a day-long supply and there is no room to paddle.

If you can find or construct a long narrow container and cover it with wire netting, you would have a very satisfactory receptacle.

Remember that ducklings, like their elders, need to immerse their beaks and swill them around.

For watering older ducklings and adults, we have several four-litre ice cream containers nailed to boards plus ice cream buckets stabilised by a surround of bricks or soil. As already mentioned, some depth is required so that eye and nasal cleanliness and hygiene can be maintained. Ducks spill a lot of water so, in winter especially, I move containers frequently or raise them on to 'duckboards' (raised, slatted wooden frames) to reduce water logging and offensive odours.

————

THE POND

Outside the night enclosure, we have a plastic baby's bath and, best of all, a small pond. Now a pond is not at all necessary to induce fertility or laying as some may suggest, but it is fun for the ducks and happy livestock are usually productive livestock. A pond is also fun for the duck keeper and it is very easy to construct.

A small pond is easy to make.

To make your pond, dig a smoothish hole 30 centimetres or a trifle deeper and in an area, maybe a minimum of 1.5 metres x 2 metres. Line this with a sheet of heavy plastic and run a line of concrete slabs, bricks or slates around the edge. The blue plastic liner in our pond is still intact and watertight after six years.

The effort put into building the pond and planting bamboo and water plants around it are repaid many times over when you see successive generations of ducklings teetering on the edge before venturing in for their maiden swim. The older ducks too, cooling themselves off and preening with such pleasure whilst gently floating about, quickly put aside your memories of digging, carting and carrying.

At least one side of your pond should be sloped more gently or rocks placed strategically so that youngsters can easily leave the water. It is a good idea also, to make one end of the pond deeper so that it is easier to empty, a chore which is necessary every 3 or 4 weeks. Duck droppings accumulate and the water turns green as the algae builds up.

Our ducks wander a long way from home. A dam, some 500 metres distant, is a favourite destination and a permanent water hole even further away is visited occasionally and their games and antics there are very absorbing. Close to our concrete water tank is a hollow which collects water from the tank when it overflows. When this occurs, the noise of the ducks can be deafening and the performance highly entertaining. I have seen a dozen ducks line up and take turns to dash towards the water hole, belly flop into it and then return, in line, for another run, all the while flapping and squealing with delight.

HYPOTHERMIA OR REDUCTION OF BODY TEMPERATURE

When you have young ducklings up to about six weeks old, you need to ensure that they can escape from any water container in which they might trap themselves. They climb in for a drink or wash and succumb to hypothermia when they are unable to clamber out; the lower the water level, the harder it is to escape. During the breeding season, I place a half a brick in the 4 litre containers and the baby bath, while with the buckets, I drape a strip of hessian over the side and fix it with half a brick so that the young'uns can claw their way out of a dangerous indiscretion. This simple precaution has saved many a young duckling, not to mention the chickens.

While on the subject of hypothermia, rain, particularly a sudden storm, can be much enjoyed by ducks, but it very quickly soaks the soft and open down of ducklings who can succumb to the cold very quickly. Bedraggled ducklings might need to be dried off and warmed before being returned to the clutch. As a rough rule, if they are preening, they can manage; if they are just standing there shivering, they need a towel and some heat. I have often saved a young bird lying on its side and apparently dead, by rushing it into the oven. Naturally, the temperature needs to be watched carefully or you will cook the unfortunate, so do not leave the stove and keep testing the heat with a thermometer or your hand. Remember that a metal dish will absorb calories at a rapid rate and scorch the patient unless you place a thick cloth under the duckling. Resurrection is nothing short of miraculous and takes about ten minutes.

One more warning about water and ducklings. Ducklings hatched under a duck will float on a pond because oil from the mother rubs off and adheres to the hatchlings' down. Ducklings hatched under a hen do not have this advantage and can become soaked to the skin if allowed near water in the first few days. Keep ducklings hatched by a hen away from water for several days until their own oil glands give them floating power.

———

5

RAISING DUCKLINGS

GENETICS / HATCHING MUSCOVIES /
SITTING / THE EVENT / HATCHING
KHAKI CAMPBELLS /WHAT YOU WILL
NEED TO DO / THE CLUCKY CHOOK /
THE MUSCOVY AS MOTHER / POST
HATCHING

We have raised hundreds of ducklings and I still find it fascinating. They can be hatched under a duck, under a hen or in an incubator and it always conjures up a warm and satisfying feeling when, after the prescribed 28 or 35 days, you approach the nest and view a writhing mass of brown or yellow down.

However, it does not always happen that way and the happening can be very wasteful if nature is left to take her own course. We must stop and remind ourselves that we are dealing with domesticated livestock where Nature has already been meddle with and so, as the meddlers, we must take our share of responsibility for what happens to our charges. Planning is certainly necessary, and sometimes, intervention as well.

GENETICS

If you want strong stock, make sure the parents are not related. If you purchase a clutch, then dispose of the males before breeding commences so that they cannot mate with their sisters. Swap one and sell or eat the rest. Inbreeding results in small ducklings, death in the shell, malformations and inherited weaknesses such as slip-wing and leg weakness.

Large ducks are likely to produce large ducklings, so select breeding stock carefully; remember that they are at their peak in the first two years. I usually replace our ducks from the best of the young ones and acquire a new drake for them. The drake can service four ducks comfortably and up to eight in his prime and he works well for 4 or 5 years at least.

———

HATCHING MUSCOVIES

The nest: Muscovies lay only to breed. When coming on to lay, the duck spends her time close to the drake, her back is seldom clean and the flesh around her head assumes a brilliant and vibrant red. She pokes around in corners assessing the suitability of nesting sites, maybe under a box or lean-to you have provided, under a bush or a pile of wood, in a corner of the duck shed or in any dark nook that takes her fancy; you might just have to watch. If she is not laying in the yard overnight, you can usually locate the nest site by following her immediately after you let her out in the morning.

The nesting site is suitable only if it can be protected from predators over the two months from first egg to hatching. Sometimes another duck covets the site and one of them has to choose again. I find, however, that the most inconvenience is caused by marauding chickens which scratch and scatter eggs and by ducklings which like to snuggle in cosy corners and could the nest, dissuading the rightful occupant from continuing her nesting arrangements there. Other ducks will lay in the same nest if sufficient sites are not available.

Ducks often return to the same site for subsequent sittings.

The duck will lay one egg per day and she usually builds her tally to about 18 eggs before sitting. When the tally reaches about twelve, I check on the shape and depth of the nest and scrape away soil, a job the duck often performs inadequately. I spread some pliable straw or dry grass on the nest and build the surround so that eggs will not roll out. It is also a good time to check for gaps and crevices through which day-olds could escape or where they might become wedged. It is worth marking some of the first laid eggs so that if the duck overflows the nest, you know which ones to remove to reduce to a 16–18 egg setting. These newer eggs will be edible and you can check by breaking them into a cup before use. Laying continues until the duck is satisfied with the quantity and if you remove a few for your own use before she begins to sit, they will be replaced.

———

SITTING

Before finally settling down, the duck usually spends a few nights practicing and then comes off during the day. Eggs need 48 hours incubation before germination commences so do not be alarmed at the thought of the eggs cooling off during the day. Most ducks pluck down from their bodies in the early days of sitting so that eggs are insulated when they leave the nest to feed and to preen. They leave the nest once or twice a day, though recently, one of ours was up and down like yo-yo and the hatching was 100% and bang on cue. Check the routine as some ducks are timid about leaving the nest during the frenzy of the feeding period and stagger out just as the last of the wheat is disappearing. Saving the siting duck some fresh greens is important. Greens are often gobbled up early in the feeding session and s the duck gets little time to browse, she will miss out altogether is she is late for meals.

Once under way, there is not much for you to do. They will turn the eggs over once each day. Occasionally she breaks and egg which she will then remove, but if it happened to be rotten, the nest will attract flies and you will need to clean it up. Eggs hatch after 35 days.

THE EVENT

At about the 30 day mark I try to be ready when she leaves the nest so that I can test the eggs by placing them in a bucket of water heated to about blood heat; 98.4 F or 37 C or a little warmer.

Any eggs which do not float should be discarded without further ado. Now the live eggs not only float, they will bob quite vigorously as the embryo changes position within the shell. Return these active eggs to the nest and give the remainder another minute and if if they still do not wriggle, they are dead. The chances are though that you will obtain an excellent hatching.

This culling is well worth while as it removes eggs which would foul the nest if broken. Also, the duck is inclined to stay longer on the nest till all the eggs have hatched, so you could save her a long and fruitless wait at a time when she should be tending the youngsters. Another problem problem occurs when all the eggs do not hatch simultaneously. The duck will stand over the newly hatched and squirming ducklings so that the temperature is not maintained sufficiently to hatch the remaining eggs. You can either transfer the ducklings to a box, warming them with a 60 watt light globe or you can transfer the eggs to an incubator at 40 C. Either way I have always found the duck willing to accept any extra bodies you can slip back under her.

In lieu of an incubator, a frypan can be used, but it is a little tricky and some preliminary research is recommended. Our frypan has a ceramic insert, and if I 1. make up a plywood and towelling base, and 2. pad the sides ands turn the thermostat to its lowest, and 3. open the lid one centimetre, then the temperature is 40 C. in the middle. It is all a little risky, still it is an option in an emergency.

The idea of tampering with nature seems to upset some people. Certainly there is now evidence enough that civilised man has tampered too much. But we do intervene to assist a cow or ewe with a difficult birth and save both dam and offspring. So why not double the number in a ducks's clutch with a little midwifery.

———

HATCHING KHAKI CAMPBELLS

Setting a Khaki Campbell duck can be a major project and wrought with complications, to wit, pushing the duck off the nest each morning and barring entrance during the day till she goes off the boil. It is just not worth it if you have some other means of natural incubation; besides, you lose an egg a day for ten weeks or more.

If you do not have a laying Muscovy and cannot acquire a broody hen, or if you have and enquiring mind or are unable to resist a challenge, then at least let me forewarn you.

A Khaki Campbell duck lays its eggs out in the yard at random or in a common nest. On the day she decides to *sit*, there could be any number of eggs under her, maybe only one, though probably not the 14 to 16 which she could straddle comfortably.

———

WHAT YOU WILL NEED TO DO

For starters, the nest needs to be checked for shape and depth or else eggs will roll out and extra eggs will need to be added to bring the setting up to strength. Keep her in the yard while making adjustments and she will return to the nest, tolerant of your interference. If you have ample nesting sites and she is aggressive in her maternity, the others may give her a wide berth, but there is a real danger that one or more in her flock will decide to sit with her. With two sitting together, eggs find their way into the cold, and extra eggs are laid, so that simultaneous hatchings then become impossible. (I have even seen a drake join in with the quarrels and commotion caused by multiple *sittings*.

If the other ducks are bothering her, your sitting duck will need to be isolated in a small enclosure, preferably out of site of the others. Provide food and water along with fresh greens daily and make sure that she has her own supply of shellgrit.The gregarious spirit is never far from the surface and four weeks is a long time for her to sublimate it. If she breaks a rotten egg and you have to clean up the nest to discourage blowflies, (which incidentally, 'blow' the duck herself) or if you want to remove an early duckling, then you will see just how flighty she can become.

Intervention can endanger eggs or young and the duck is often so protective of her young that they are difficult to tame. All this makes it even more important to test the eggs in the water bucket on the 24th to 25th day. At this time you can still chase her off the nest. If you need to work under a sitting duck, us a light plywood or masonite board, about 20 x 30 cms, to slip between her and your exploring fingers. It is amazing what she will allow you to do if she cannot see it happening.

———

THE CLUCKY CHOOK

The clucky or broody hen will sit happily for four weeks and will mother ducklings well. It is a good idea idea to rub anti-lice powder into her beforehand, otherwise she might decamp if irritation becomes unbearable. She may not return until she has dust bathed, a process which could take several hours, not serious on a warm day late in the cycle, but dicey in the first two weeks.

THE MUSCOVY AS MOTHER

I often set Khaki Campbell eggs under a Muscovy with excellent results. On several occasions, though, ducks have left the young after several days; whether the maternal instinct gave out or it was because of racial discrimination, I shall never know. Interestingly, the ducklings hatched and raised this way are, more often than not, quieter and easier to manage than when raised by a mother of their own breed.

The author attending his flock.

POST HATCHING

I always try to isolate a mother with her ducklings for between 4 and 7 days. The ducklings become bonded to the right duck, handy if several clutches become boxed or locked in together. This ensures that with mother's help, they get the best food and are not left with just the scraps. They are well protected from predators, including hawks and children and they do not become lost.

When moving a clutch for the first time (in the interests of hygiene, this should be done on the day after the hatching), drive the ducklings and the mother together for she will return to the nest repeatedly, looking for strays. If it is safe to do so, leave her at the nest until she sallies forth with the youngsters. The problem is that hatchlings can be trampled either when they go exploring or by ducks milling around the nest, who may be just curious of looking for chick-bits

You can set up a temporary fence as protection, though sometimes a mother can show pure genius in escaping from the enclosure. (For instance, she could make a considerable effort to leave the nest to defecate and with good reason, as a duck can build up quite a head of steam in the final days before hatching when she seldom leaves the nest.) Whatever protection you install, it must be escape proof if for no other reason the the duck's complete ineptitude in regaining the nest after having escaped.

Mother and hatchlings enjoy a little privacy.

Khaki Campbell ducklings are much more timid than Muscovies. They scare easily and if one scares they all move in concert. One alarm squeak from Mum and they are totally docile, but at this point you have already been labelled as hostile, a reputation which is difficult to live down. I'll talk more about taming later.

———

6

HATCHING IN THE INCUBATOR

THE EGG SETTING / THE INCUBATOR / TESTING, DAMPING AND TURNING / HATCHING IN THE INCUBATOR / FEEDING / PROBLEMS / HOUSING THE MOTHERLESS BROOD

I use a small 3 dozen egg incubator. With both duck and hen eggs, I have managed, at best only a 1/3 hatchings, but when I planted the eggs under a duck for 10–14 days and then switched them to the incubator, a good 80–90% hatching rate was achieved regularly. Eggs can be returned to the duck just before hatching and the setting under her can be transferred to the incubator: you double production, but eventually you have to be mother.

THE EGG SETTING

Muscovy eggs are usually well shaped, and smooth and biscuit colour and except for those from the novice, are of a good size. If you are selecting Khaki Campbell eggs, discard the very small, the very large and the misshapen; also the pointed eggs which restrict movement during hatching. Strong shells have a smooth feel, while weaker shells are slightly chalky to the touch. Drakes and ducks should not be related as inbreeding causes poor hatchings and produce weaker ducklings.

THE INCUBATOR

For successful hatching in the incubator it is necessary that you should be methodical and learn all you can about the machine. A few pointers here are in order.

- First read the instruction which accompany the machine.
- Take plenty of time, 24 hours at least, to regulate the machine.
- Remove the egg-turner normally used for hen eggs; duck eggs can be placed flat on the wire tray.
- Yolks could burst if cold eggs are shut in the machine straightaway so introduce the eggs and leave the door open for 3 to 4 hours so that they warm gradually.
- Make sure the water tray is filled.
- I have found that the most successful temperature setting in our still-air incubator is 40°C (or 103.5°F). This is crucial, as 38.6°C (101.5°F) is the average as the temperature rises and falls as the lamp switches on and off. Other breeders with different, and perhaps more accurate machines prefer lower settings. Some even change the setting moving up each week starting at 38.6°C (101.5°F) and increasing to 39°C (102.2°F), then 39.5°C (103.1°F) for the last two weeks. Another, who adds a few eggs each week rather than fill the incubator with one setting, keeps rigidly to 39°C (102.2°F). (In a forced-air machine, the heat is distributed constantly and evenly around the eggs so that slightly lower temperatures are in order.
- Keep an ordinary 100 watt bulb on hand in case the lamp fails.
- If a blackout occurs, wrap the whole tray in a

sleeping bag or eiderdown. This will maintain the temperature for several hours at least.

- If the eggs have cooled down, plunge them in very warm water, just cool enough to put your hand in. Keep them there for 3 or 4 minutes, then keep them warm until you have brought the incubator up to 40°C again.
- The temperature in the incubator will vary with hot days and cold nights and also when you vary the humidity. It shouldn't but it does.
- Both late and early hatchings are usually the result of temperature variations.

TESTING, DAMPING AND TURNING

Water in the incubator tray boosts humidity, but the fan has a drying effect. Feel under a duck on the nest and you will know just how damp the eggs should be. I place our in water twice a day; water temperature is at blood heat or a little more and immersion is for about one minute.

In the early days the eggs sink; then one by one they float. This occurs at a week or 10 days before hatching then the eggs begin to bob around in the water, very gently at first and then quite violently just prior to hatching. Immersion keeps the shells soft, and it is exciting to monitor the development of the embryos (dead eggs can be detected and discarded).

I mark each side of the eggs, one side with a line and one with a circle so that it is always quite clear as to which eggs I have turned. Turning should take place twice a day, as near to every 12 hours as is convenient. It is handy to have several wood strips or pieces of material to prevent eggs rolling on the tray.

HATCHING IN THE INCUBATOR

When cheeps can be heard, hatching is not far off, about 48 hours. Shells are pipped within 24 hours and hatching takes place in the following 24 hours.

Eggs which fail to open but from which you detect activity can be pipped, but the young still die in the shell. Maybe the stock was weak or inbred, but probably the temperature or the humidity was too low. Half a degree variation from the correct temperature can effect the process.

———

TWO PROBLEMS

Firstly, if the humidity is low when hatching commences, the fan can dry out the down on the duckling and cause it to stick to the shell. Secondly, if the temperature falls, so does the activity displayed by the duckling. It continues to grow, but after pipping the shell, it is unable to turn in the egg and chip away the remainder of the circle of shell and force its way out.

If, after 24 hours from pipping of the shell you fear for the bird, chip off the top of the egg, at the blunt end then crack the shell lengthways. Unravel the head gently, free any down which has stuck to the shell and then return it to the incubator. *Do not separate* the duckling from the pointed end of the shell. An umbilical cord connects the baby's anus or cloaca to the shell and it must be allowed to whither away in its own time over the next hour or two.

If your intervention was timely, a moist young duckling will emerge smoothly from the shell. If you are too quick, blood will be evident and maybe an anal bulge or prolapse. All is not lost, and provided you have not severed the umbilical cord, the will probably receded within twelve hours. If not or if the youngster is in pain, indicated by cheeps or by flutterings of the wings or legs, or if it does not sit up next morning, then kill it—off with its head and no further painful delays.

Leave the duckling in the incubator until they are sitting up, fluffed out and active, probably after several hours, but an overnight stay will do no harm. Birds are born well supplied with food and can manage well for 24 hours without extra sustenance. Remember the humidity is eliminated if the water surface is covered and this occurs rapidly when a newly hatched bird sheds numerous specks of powdery down, so replenish the water in the tray frequently.

I might hatch a complete clutch in the incubator or a few eggs the duck seems to be neglecting. Once hatched, the ducklings can be slipped under the mother; use the board mentioned earlier if she seems cantankerous. She will accept extra ducklings from the incubator over the next couple of days and I have had a duck nurturing up to 24 young ones, quite a sight when she steers them to the pond for the first time. Twenty-four would be too many in cold weather unless the whole family were very well sheltered.

The duck accepts extra ducklings because she cannot count but if you introduce a duckling of a different colour, she will spurn it and chase it from the nest. On the other hand, she will happily accept ducklings of a different colour if she has hatched them herself, so a white Aylesbury or Pekin hatching out with Khaki Campbells will be tended.

———

HOUSING THE MOTHERLESS BROOD

If you have incubated ducklings and are required to play mother, then the first thing is to provide accommodation. After hatching, the birds need a brooder or a box and lamp for warmth. This is not difficult to provide. The home brooder shown here is suitable for 12 to 15 ducklings. Here are a few points to remember.

- The box needs to be draught-free. This means keeping it indoors for at least a week, longer in cold weather.
- The box should allow access to a small run where food and water are provided.
- The flooring could be sawdust, shavings, shredded paper, rice hulls or even kitty litter. There is no need to clean it out during the week or so that you house the ducklings there; just top it up every day or so and perhaps replace wet shavings around the water reservoir.
- A table top provides extra safety and also an excellent viewing, though the floor is fine.
- A fence around the box and the run would need to be 400 mm high to keep the birds in and higher and stronger if necessary to exclude predators such as children, dogs and cats.
- The ducklings need to be supplied with warmth for at least a week and up to a fortnight while nights are cold.

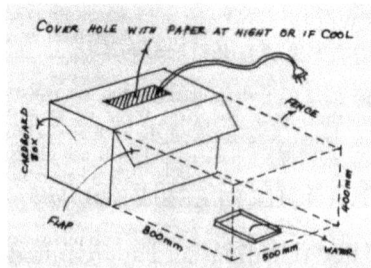

A suggested design for a home made brooder.

- For heating, hang a light bulb just above head hight

and test the floor temperature with a thermometer. A 30°C would be ideal to start with. If the ducklings are cold, they will huddle together under the lamp; if they are hot, they will be scattered away from the bulb. To adjust the temperature, raise or lower the light bulb and adjust the covering over the whole in the top of the box and rearrange the front flap. Always leave an opening so that the ducklings can get to the food and water.

• Adjusting the temperature over the week gradually hardens them for an outside life.

• When eventually you move them to an outside shed at night, provide them with a box and bag flap. You will often find that you need to herd them into the box, as the campsite they select at dusk can become a cold spot by early morning.

• Young birds tend to crowd each other into corners so, if you have more than a dozen ducklings, it is a good idea to round off the corners inside their sleeping quarters; corrugated cardboard does the job well.

FEEDING

As mentioned earlier under the heading *Feeding Ducklings*, chick-bits or crumbles are a must for the hatchlings. Now that you are their mother, there are a couple of extra feeding points to mention.

• Even though I provide feed and water in the run outside the box, on the first day I scatter crumbles over a small board which I locate near the light bulb. The ducklings will peck at anything which stands out

from the surroundings. I also induce feeding by
sprinkling a few crumbles over the backs of the
ducklings. This produces an instant response.

- The all-important water will sometimes seem
  ignored. If I think I need to introduce ducklings to
  water, I just hold their heads over a glass of water
  and push their beaks in.
- A few blades of grass floating on the water ensures
  the ducklings will see it. Being naturally inquisitive,
  they will notice the slightest movement on the water
  and investigate.
- Whatever else you do, never let them run out of
  water.

———

7

OF MANY THINGS

SEXING DUCKLINGS / A BIRD FOR THE
TABLE / COOKING / CATCHING AND
HANDLING / TRANSPORTING /
SICKNESS AND INJURY / DUCKS AND
YOUNG CHILDREN

SEXING DUCKLINGS

I have not tried it, but experts tell me it is so, that if you take a fully fluffed out day-old duckling, before it has consumed food or water, and part the cloaca or vent, you might see the penis, a pinkish root tip which would be absent in the female. The trouble is that they wriggle so much and I give up.

With Khaki Campbells, if you are content to wait till the birds are about three-quarters feathered, then pick up each duck; females will quack and the males will hiss. Up to this stage sexing is by no means reliable. If I am asked to select females from a clutch of youngsters, I pick out those with the blackest beaks. The greenish-beaked birds are more often males, but this is by no means certain, particularly in the lighter-coloured birds.

With Muscovies, the males are larger, they have bigger feet and their beak line runs straight back over a receding forehead, while the female has a curved and more aesthetic headline.

A BIRD FOR THE TABLE

Khaki Campbells are supposed to be mature by 12 to 14 weeks, Muscovy drakes at 16 weeks and females at 14 weeks. To kill them before maturity will give you a carcass with a higher bone percentage. The trick is to pluck them when there are no tiny pin feathers; removal of these can prolong the plucking operation almost beyond endurance. Pin feathers, it seems, grow on Muscovy drakes in both the 15th and 17th weeks. I have found it better to leave them several weeks. Though they are supposed to be mature, I find that they still have a kilo of growing to do and the wait saves hours of plucking time. The advice might not be economic for a commercial grower, hence the advice to kill at 16 weeks.

I kill with an axe and, as soon as the blood flow staunches, dip the carcass in water for two minutes a temperature of 65°C to 70°C, i.e. hot tap temperature. Several tablespoons of detergent helps the water percolate through the oily feathers and softens the skin. I move the body around vigorously and use a flat stick to ruffle the feathers all over.

Cooler water makes for harder plucking, but if the duck is in water which is too hot for too long, fat is brought to the surface and produces a yellow skin; this does not effect the taste, but some people prefer the traditional white carcass.

————

COOKING

A 16 week Muscovy drake will weigh in at just over 3 kilos, an older drake at closer to 4 kilos, ducks and Khaki Campbells a little over 2 kilos. These weights are for standard strains. The secret is to cook slowly in a low oven. Use a roasting bag or baste frequently. Allow 40 to 50 minutes per kilo at 190°C. Ducks older than six months become decreasingly suitable for roasting, but are just as tasty out of a casserole.

———

CATCHING AND HANDLING

Unless catching and handling is absolutely necessary, *don't* , and then always slowly. All movements need to be measured and as predictable as possible Noise is not upsetting, but scary motions will send them scattering timorously in all directions. When herding them, they are most fond of playing 'silly fellas', particularly if there are tree trunks or other obstacles en route. It is a good idea to have a nearby stick or two. They see these as an extension of your arms and become much more amenable to directions.

To catch, herd the group into a corner; I have an old door pushed into a corner and on its side to form a wedge. I have a piece of wire, 1.5 metres in length , U-shaped at one end and twisted to that I can grasp it comfortable at the other. I slip the U around the neck of the duck I wish to catch and draw it gently towards me. The bird is then pressed firmly onto the ground until I can manage to hold it in both hands, wings held against the body and the vent of the duck pointed away from my legs.

Picking up a bird by the neck does not injure it in any way and holding by the wings, close to the body, is allowable, but handling ducks by the is absolutely forbidden. The leg is the part of the duck most prone to injury; one twist and the leg is damaged.

I keep herding, and certainly handling, to a minimum. It upsets the ducks, and their confidence, once eroded, is difficult to regain. If I have to catch, I make some attempt to isolate the ones I want, though sometimes it is easier to herd the lot. If killing, I certainly wield an axe away from the eyes of the flock.

TRANSPORTING

Your ducks should be transported in a well-ventilated box or wire crate. Allow them plenty of room, particularly on a warm day. Ducks generate and enormous amount of heat and collapse and die in less than twenty minutes from heat exhaustion. Transporting birds in a bag or in the boot of a car is illegal.

———

SICKNESS AND INJURY

Diseases are not common in ducks and this book is not meant to cover them; however, just a few words. If a bird is ill internally, there is not much you can do. Certainly, check with a vet if you are worried that an infection might run through the flock, but 'kill early' is a good rule. Duck diseases are not transmitted to humans so it is permissible to eat the patient. It is much better than allowing the animal to live in pain or waste away to a slow death.

Injured legs are difficult to treat, especially with the active and sociable Khaki Campbells. Try isolation for a few days on a soft surface, such as shavings, but if that does not work, then a prognosis is very poor. I suggest the axe immediately. A Muscovy is much more likely to respond and it is not unusual to have a healthy 'lumpy' in the flock whereas the brown ducks have this urge to follow the flock and any leg damage is soon exacerbated.

Ducklings can be hurt easily; I guess the wonder is that so many survive being stood on so many times. The duck will often eject a sick duckling from the nest but if the young clutch is penned during the first week, you have a good chance to check on the progress of injuries. When you realise that you need to act, then don't muck about. Do it!

DUCKS AND YOUNG CHILDREN

Many parents purchase ducks or a clutch of young'uns because 'it would be nice for the children'. Now ducks are not good pets in the cuddly sense that children understand; and some children are in the predator class. I am all in favour of encouraging children to take up birds, but they do need to be taught and trained to look after them. I suggest that with the first clutch, you make it clear that the ducklings are yours and that the children can help if they learn to do it your way. They can graduate to ownership and even make pocket money when they have learnt the way things should be done.

Every child under 8 years old who has visited us has chased ducks. The drill is to explain that the ducks become very frightened if chased and that, if they are upset, the most dire repercussions will ensure. Five minutes later you go outside and roar at the visitors. They then vehemently deny that they were chasing ducks; 'We were just walking behind them'.

———

AFTERWORD

I have said that you can expect ducks to lay their first eggs at anything from eight months on. Some of our young Khaki Campbells have just produced their maiden contributions to their upkeep at 18 weeks; mighty small eggs mind you, but eggs nevertheless. When the unexpected happens and we cannot dream up an explanation, we say, 'It's the season.' Well, maybe this time it is; three new Muscovies are sitting on eggs at no more than six months and our pullets are laying as well, at 18 weeks. I wish it happened every year.

There is a thunderstorm myth; this tantrum of nature is supposed to be instant death to ducklings in the shell. Now maybe it is lethal at a particular stage in the development of the embryo, but neither I, nor several breeder I have asked, can recall any instance when the blame for poor hatching can be sheeted home to this occurrence, either because it is noise or electrical.

I have repeated that Khaki Campbells are highly social animals. One morning, I was down the paddock and heard some particularly raucous quacking coming from beyond the house. This cacophony was so prolonged that I went to investigate. One duck was lying dead on the road and all her mates were lining the asphalt and screaming in an apparent mourning ritual. I picked up the dead bird and buried her and the noise subsided, but the whole flock fled every time I approached and not till the next morning were they back to normal.

Muscovies also have a strong affinity for those in their clan. I bought three Muscovy sisters during Spring. These three grazed together and laid and nested at the same time. (One produced a clutch which I sold, together with mum, to a young chap on a farm not far away. Unfortunately, that duck and all her young were incinerated during the bad bush fires the following year.)

I sold the second clutch to another farmer who borrowed the duck till such times as the ducklings could fend for themselves.

Some weeks later he returned her and I witnessed a most unusual event. The other Muscovies emerged from under bushes and around corners and gathered around her in welcome, with neck arching and duck noises. Then, from the circle, the remaining sister came slowly forward and, emitting low sibilant hisses, the two entwined their necks and, for five minutes, they stroked and mewed in a most touching display of love and joy whilst the others stood around, understanding and approving. Then, they all moved off to graze together and I was glad of this rare glance into my ducks and their feelings for each other.

———

Publishers note: In the first 1990 printing, the author listed numerous references in the back pages of this book. While some are still in print, the internet will now provide you with a wealth of information and book titles. For the fancier who would like to explore further and even raise ducks for showing, we recommend The BRITISH POULTRY STANDARD. It is the oldest poultry fancy breed standard in the world.

RICHARD LEE PUBLISHING

Fiction

Australian Short Stories by Richard Lee
ISBN - 978-0-909431-00-6

Restless: A novel about two young men growing up in Australia between 1900 and 1936 by Richard Lee (Publication late 2022.)

Memoir

The Kite Makers: Six years of a child's war - Britain 1939-1945 by Anita Sinclair.
ISBN - 978-0-909431-16-7

Reference

Ducks for Starters: A Practical Guide to Backyard Duck Keeping by Bruce Wicking
ISBN - 978-0-909431 - 18-1

———

Out of Print Titles

Mathematics for Young Children by Helen Western
ISBN - 978-0-909431-01-3

Currajong: For Those Whom Schools Have Failed
by Bruce Wicking
ISBN - 978-0-909431-03-7

Let Them Run a Little: Introduction to Open
Approach Learning by Bruce Wicking
ISBN - 0-90943-1000

The Puppetry Handbook by Anita Sinclair
ISBN - 978-0-909431-04-4

Wordswork by Chris Davidson & Bruce Wicking
ISBN - 978-0-909431-06-8

Sheep Production by Murray Elliott
ISBN - 978-0-909431-07-5

Sweethearts - A novel by Colin Talbot
ISBN - 978-1-875207-02-2

———

Publisher Contact

Address Rights or Book Production enquiries to:
Richard Lee Publishing, Maldon 3463 Australia.
Contact: countrynotebook@gmail.com